To Kem,

Congratulations on this your graduation from High School. May the future hold great happiness and success as you go on to college.

We're very, very proud of you!

Love

Mom & Dad

Secrets to Share

Secrets To Share

Experiences of Courage and Faith in the Lives of Famous Men and Women

Selected by Lois Daniel
Illustrated by James Hamil

♛ Hallmark Editions

CONTENTS

WITH FAITH AND COURAGE, 4

WHAT WE MAKE IT, 27

NO MAN IS AN ISLAND, 43

With Faith And Courage

THE COURAGEOUS HOSTESS

Pearl Buck's mother, a young woman with two small children, was left in the family home in China while her husband was away. The townspeople, who had suffered a long summer without rain, blamed their lack of food and crops on her and her family—the strangers who had offended their gods. She faced their anger with an inner reserve of strength and courage:

One day dawned even more sultry than the rest. The sky was white-hot and not a breath stirred the dying leaves on the bamboos in the garden. She knew that this was the day, she told me years later. She could feel the menace that hung over the silence in the city. The streets were empty, and not even the children shouted in play.

4

Late that afternoon her amah [nanny for the children] came to her in terror. "Mistress," she whispered, "they are coming tonight to kill you and the children . . . ."

At that moment, my mother said, peace came into her heart and mind. The day drew to its end and she understood what she must do. Quietly she fed the children. Then she bathed them and put on their best clothes. She dressed herself in her simple best and brushed her hair well. All this time the amah helped her but in complete amazement. What was this white woman about to do? Did she plan to kill herself and the children? Meantime the silence in the streets had broken. An ominous roar took its place. My mother knew that a mob was gathering and attack was imminent.

"Set out all our tea bowls and make fresh tea," she directed the cook. "Put the small cakes you made yesterday on plates and any fruit that we have as well."

To the gardener she said, "Open the gates of the compound—open them wide!"

They were all amazed, she told me, but she insisted and they obeyed. Then she herself opened the door of the house and she and the children sat in the main room, they with their toys and she with her sewing. They were not frightened, for she showed no fear.

6

The mob howled in the streets. They surged through the open gates, carrying sticks and knives. She put down her sewing, and when they crowded in the door of the house, she said, "Come in, come in and drink tea. I have been expecting you. You are welcome."

The men stared at her calm, smiling face. They took in the scene, the children playing and unafraid, the lamplit room, the tea and food on the table. My mother was pouring tea as she urged them to come in. She prattled on, telling them that her husband was not at home, that she was alone here with her good servants and the children.

They came in, uncertain and dazed, and the children, accustomed to the usually kind Chinese, left their toys and came to them without fear. My mother gave them tea, careful to hold each bowl in both hands in courtesy to guests.

"What happened then?" I always asked this question, breathless with suspense, though I knew the story well because I wanted often to hear it.

"They drank the tea and ate the cakes," she replied. "Not at once of course, but bit by bit. They watched the children. Then everybody went away."

"Why?"

"I don't know."

"Were you afraid?"

"I was sick with fear."

7

"Then how did you have such courage?"

"From despair."

That is what she always said. The courage came from despair.

'I FOUND MY ROCK'

At the dawn of a promising young career, actress Ann Blyth, confronted with a crisis, established her faith. Here she describes the ordeal from icy beginning to inspiring conclusion:

When I was a very little girl I remember praying fervently for a pair of red wings. After several days of watching and waiting, I took my shaken faith and spread it out before my mother.

"Why?" I demanded. "Why don't I get red wings?"

My mother had, skillfully balanced with her sensitive Irish wit, an enormous respect for a serious problem. Together we examined mine. "Faith, my darling," she told me, "is believing that God is very wise. Wiser than you. Somehow you must be praying wrong."

As I grew older I was filled with gratitude that I need not walk through life wearing red wings. But, I was equally grateful for her gentle lesson. . . .

She dreamed dreams about my wonderful future

as an actress, and at eight, nine and ten, I began getting radio and stage bits. When I tried for something better and failed, she would smile her wonderful warm smile, put a pert new feather in my hat, and together we'd go to St. Boniface's to pray.

"Just have faith, my darling," she'd say cheerfully as we walked home in the fading light. "Something better will come." And it did. It came so fast it was like riding a giant roller coaster clear to the top. We two looked out over the whole world. At thirteen I was on Broadway as Paul Lukas' daughter in "Watch on the Rhine." At fourteen I had dinner at the White House. At fifteen I came to Hollywood and was given the coveted role of Joan Crawford's daughter in "Mildred Pierce." Overnight life was glamorous, exciting, completely wonderful.

Yes, we went up so fast that when we hit the first giant dip it shook my faith. But it didn't shake my mother's on that tragic day in a hospital room, where doctors told me I might never walk again.

We had finished "Mildred Pierce" and Mother took a group of us to Snow Valley, a spot in the San Bernardino Mountains. While my friends and I were tobogganing, it happened. One minute we were sailing down the hard-packed icy hillside like snow birds, then there was a crash and I fell on my back with a sickening thud.

I didn't cry out. The feeling was too big for that.

Involuntarily, from long habit, my spirit reached out for faith and halting prayers rose to my lips. At the hospital the doctors were grave; my back was broken.

My glowing world tumbled all about me! It seemed like the end of everything.

At first I couldn't look at my mother. When at last I raised my head, I was startled. Those warm hazel eyes under her crown of auburn hair were actually smiling.

"Have faith, my darling," she said. "You'll walk."

Together my mother and I planned cheerful, busy days. In a cast, with my head and feet toward the floor, my back raised high, I concentrated on high school work, determined to graduate with my studio class.

But still there were those long periods of just lying there. The busy exciting world I had known faded away and my life slowed down to little things. But even here I found myself blessed, for a new sense of prayer began to unfold to me. Now there were not the busy times of telling Him what I needed, but rather times of listening communion, of gathering strength, when my human strength and courage seemed to ebb away.

In seven months they told me I could walk. Not walk really, but take those first important few steps on the long road back to complete freedom. As I had gotten to know Him in my time of trial, I knew Him now in thanksgiving.

I took those steps, and then more. I graduated with my class from a wheel chair.

There were seven months in and out of that wheel chair, but every one was another step forward. There was my first swim. The preview of "Mildred Pierce." My first game of golf. And then I made my first picture since the accident.

Now, at last, life was again the same. Only, not quite the same. I found within me an immense gratitude for simple things. An acute appreciation of all I might have lost, all the things I had accepted unconsciously before. And one more difference, I had grown up. At first I had clung to my mother's faith, leaned on her; step by step she showed me the way. Now, I had found my own rock. Nor did I find it too soon.

A SUPPORT BEYOND ONESELF

Singer Marian Anderson expresses her sentiments on prayer and religion in her book, My Lord, What a Morning. *Here she tells where she found "new strength" when she needed it:*

Good habits can be fine things. If you say your prayers every night there comes a time when they grow more meaningful to you. The child who learns to repeat after his mother, "Now I lay me down to sleep," may get a little thrill out of just saying it, at the beginning. After a time he realizes that he can do nothing about keeping his own soul when he is asleep. As he says, "Now I lay me down to sleep, I pray Thee, Lord, my soul to keep," the realization comes to him that there is Someone else to whom he can commit his soul when he cannot take care of it himself.

And later, when Mother taught us the Lord's Prayer, she put her heart into it. You tried to say it as she did, and you had to put a little of your own heart into it. I believe that Mother, realizing that she was left alone to raise three girls, knew that she had to have a support beyond herself. . . .

I may have had moments of being too preoccupied with immediate affairs to think of larger matters. But as I grew older I saw that talking to Mother helped me when I was in trouble, and then I realized, as I traveled and was away from home for long periods, that I could not always count on reaching out to her for support. The time came when I had to decide where I would find the new strength I needed. I found it where Mother had always found hers. . . .

My religion is something I cherish. I am not in church every Sunday, but I hope and believe that I am on good speaking terms with Him. I carry my

troubles, and I don't sit back waiting for them to be cleared up. I realize that when the time is ripe they will be dissolved, but I don't mean that one should sit inert, waiting for all things to come from above. If one has a certain amount of drive, intelligence, and conscientiousness, one must use them. Having made the best effort, one is more likely to get a hearing in an extremity.

'WE ARE GRATEFUL'

Actress Helen Hayes reminds us of the importance of daily prayer in this selection from her book, A Gift of Joy:

I think it is unfortunately true of a great many men and women today that though they believe in God they do not feel the need to speak or, if you will, pray to Him. Prayer, a rabbi has said, is a "ladder reaching from earth to heaven, from man to God" and without prayer no religion is truly alive.

I know that we are told that every good thought we have and everything we do that is good is actually in itself a prayer; that everything we do that is imbued with kindness or love for others is our simple and sincere way of telling God that we are grateful for what good we have from Him. I know this is true, but I don't think it is enough. It reminds me of

14

the story of the lazy man who had his secretary or someone else copy a whole lot of prayers for him which he had pinned up on the wall of his bedroom, and, when it was time to pray, he would just point to one and say, "Lord, them's my sentiments."

There is a certain value in the discipline of saying the formal prayers that have been created by inspired men. As an actress I have known the value of discipline since childhood. I have been taught that each performance must be fresh and good and you must never relax or let down. This sense of discipline also comes from my Catholic upbringing. As Rabbi Robert Gordis observed in his *A Faith for Moderns*, "Even if the goal of true communion with God is achieved only intermittently, it justifies the discipline, the routine, even the long periods when the heart is silent though the lips move, when God seems absent though His name is repeated time and again." Gordis continues with a marvelous parable once told by the Rabbi of Rizin:

"In a small village the only watchmaker died, and because the population was small, no new craftsman came to take his place. As time went on, watches and clocks began to lose and gain time, and no accurate timepieces remained. Some villagers accordingly let their watches run down, while others doggedly kept winding theirs each day, though their accuracy left much to be desired. Some time later, a wandering watchmaker came to town, and all the villagers rushed to bring their timepieces for repair. Those watches that had been allowed to run down were beyond repair, for their mechanisms had rusted. The lesson is clear. The spiritual life must be guarded against merely perfunctory exercise, to be sure, but even the routine performance serves as a necessary discipline and the prelude to great moments of exaltation open to every man."

'HIS WILL'

Author Catherine Marshall financed her future with faith. In this selection from her book, Beyond Ourselves, *she describes how:*

Perhaps one reason that the real meaning of faith eluded me personally for so many years was that it is so surprisingly simple, so practical. Faith in God is simply trusting Him enough to step out on trust.

My first lesson in stepping out on trust came in connection with the problem of financing a college education. We were then living in a little railroad town in the eastern panhandle of West Virginia. By the time I reached my senior year in high school, the town had for some years been struggling through the long aftermath of the 1929 crash. Its only industry—the Baltimore and Ohio railroad shops—were all but shut down. The church my father served as minister was suffering along with everything else. Father had voluntarily taken several cuts in his already meager salary. Even grocery money was scarce. It was fortunate that Mother knew how to prepare fried mush in a way that made it seem like a rare delicacy.

Something I had dreamed of as far back as I could remember—a college education—now seemed out of the question. The dream even included a particular college—Agnes Scott in Decatur, Georgia.

Agnes Scott accepted me. Although the school was accustomed to ministers' and missionaries' daughters whose ambitions outstripped their pocketbooks, the financial burden nevertheless looked hopelessly heavy. Even with the promise of a small work scholarship and the $125 I had saved from high school essay and debating prizes, we were several hundred dollars short.

It was frightening to see that my parents were helpless in this situation. It was in their faces, in their voices. Through all my growing-up years, in every childish emergency they had been equal to anything. What now? Did this mean that I was going to have to relinquish my heart's desire?

One evening Mother found me lying across my bed, sobbing. She sat down beside me, put her cool hand on my forehead. No words were needed. She knew what the trouble was.

Presently she said quietly, "You and I are going to pray about this. Let's go into the guest room where we won't be disturbed." And she took me firmly by the hand.

We sat down on the old-fashioned golden-oak bed, the one that Mother and Father had bought for their first home. "Let's talk about this a minute before we pray," Mother said slowly. "I believe that it is God's will for you to go to college, or else He would not have given you the mental equipment. Furthermore, all resources are at God's disposal. Do you believe that, Catherine?"

"Yes—yes—I think I do."

"All right. Now here's another fact I want you to think about. Everybody has faith. We're born with it. Much of what happens to us in life depends on where we place our faith. If we deposit it in God, then we're on sure ground. If we place our trust in poverty or failure or fear, then we're investing it poorly. So keep that in mind while I read something to you." She opened a Moffatt Bible to I John 5:14, 15:

Now the confidence we have in Him is this,
that He listens to us whenever we ask anything
in accordance with His will; and if we know
that He listens to whatever we ask, we know
that we obtain the requests we have made to Him.

"Note how the thought goes in that promise, Catherine. Whenever we ask God for something that is His will, He hears us. If He hears us, then He grants the request we have made. So you and I can rest on that promise. Let's claim it right now for the resources for your college." And so we knelt by the bed and prayed about it.

I shall never forget that evening. During those quiet moments in the bedroom, I was learning what faith is and how it works. It is true that my faith was immature and weak, but the strength of Mother's was contagious. She had helped me take my first step in faith. The answer would come. We knew it would, though neither of us had any idea how.

When it came, it was the offer of a job for Mother with the Federal Writer's Project. Would she be willing to write the history of the county? Would she! Her salary would cover the amount needed for my college expenses with a little to spare. Since history has always been one of Mother's loves, no job could have been more to her liking. Moreover, she could work at home and, along with her writing, keep a hand on all of the family projects.

That was the way I learned that we must have faith *before* the fact, not after, if we are to function as human beings at all. The only question is—faith in whom? Faith in what?

God challenges us to place it in Him rather than in

fallible human beings: "Taste and see that the Lord is good." In my experience this is not an ivory-tower approach. It is the only effectual one.

'I STILL BELIEVE'

Amidst death and despair in Nazi Germany, young Anne Frank had the courage to maintain her faith in mankind:

It's really a wonder that I haven't dropped all my ideals, because they seem so absurd and impossible to carry out. Yet I keep them, because in spite of everything I still believe that people are really good at heart. I simply can't build up my hopes on a foundation consisting of confusion, misery, and death. I see the world gradually being turned into a wilderness, I hear the ever-approaching thunder which will destroy us too, I can feel the sufferings of millions and yet, if I look up into the heavens, I think that it will all come right, that this cruelty too will end, and that peace and tranquillity will return again.

In the meantime, I must uphold my ideals, for perhaps the time will come when I shall be able to carry them out.

'THE HOUSE IN WHICH
WE LIVED'

The struggles of life require belief. In her book,
Living by Faith, *Faith Baldwin discusses the importance and individuality of believing:*

My faith has been sorely tried at times, in which I'm no different from the vast majority of people . . . but, except for one black period long ago, which lasted for some months, it has never failed me for more than a few minutes or hours at a time.

Occasionally people write me in despair and desperation; they have lost everything, they tell me, including faith. What are they to do about it?

These letters are very difficult to answer because there is no formula. . . . And you can't, with a good conscience, reply in terms of clichés, banalities, generalities, with your pen or typewriter ribbon immersed in inky soothing syrup. Emergence from darkness into light is a personal victory; how you accomplish it is up to you. You have, of course, if you look for it, help from other people who love you. But the ultimate conquering is your own affair. One person's way of solving a problem might not be your way or mine.

There are, in Australia, mines where the brown coal is on the surface, though most mines are underground. I think of one's personal faith as a mine,

sometimes on the surface, open to the sun and yielding readily the material for warmth and comfort; at
other times underground, far in the depths of one's
personal self, tunneled deep and dimly lighted;
sometimes not lighted at all. Then you have to dig
for it.

Faith is a hard core of inner sustenance. It is a tall
tree with tremendous, deep roots. It is the house in
which we live. Sometimes the core is hard to find;
sometimes the tree is shaken with wind or struck by
lightning; and sometimes we forget or mislay the
key to the house. But faith is an attitude of mind, a
quality of heart, and a spiritual benefaction. Without it we are homeless, destroyed, and starved.

Faith can be weakened by dwelling on past errors
and unhappiness; it can be made stronger by the
present struggle, and always it can join hands with
its little sister, Hope, looking toward the future.

It was kind of my parents to name me Faith; it has
given me something to try to live up to, although for
many years I did not recognize this challenge.

It costs me something to admit that, even now, I
fall easily into the dreamy state known as wishful
thinking. This is not faith—it isn't even a close rela-
tive of Hope; perhaps a second cousin once removed?
And I know better than to think wishfully. I know
I can't sit with my hands folded and wish myself
into better situations or solutions, or wish myself

out of certain circumstances. For these alterations I must work, and while I am working, although I can draw courage from hope, I must depend upon faith.

BEAUTIFUL COURAGE

The late journalist and author Dorothy Thompson writes about courage in her book, The Courage To Be Happy. *Here she comments on a phrase used by Joseph Joubert, a French writer during the Napoleanic era, in a letter to his beloved Pauline de Beaumont:*

"One must learn to love life . . ." he insisted. "I am well content to tell you that I cannot admire you at leisure, and hold you in high esteem as I would wish, until I perceive in you the most beautiful of all forms of courage, the courage to be happy."

At this point I am content to leave Joubert and his Pauline—who did not become his, but fell in love with his friend and rival, the eminent Chateaubriand —to ponder what seems to me a remarkable phrase, "The courage to be happy." For never before had it occurred to me that it required courage to be happy, or that happiness is a demonstration of courage. Courage had always seemed to me to be that quality of mind that faces danger without fear, or endures pain, disappointment, grief, or loss with fortitude. I had thought of it, indeed, as the spirit that bravely endures *un*happiness.

But no. For M. Joubert, whom his biographers recognize as an exceedingly rare human spirit, the boy standing on the burning deck, valorous though he was, did not exhibit the most *beautiful* form of courage, nor all the unflinching burden-bearers whose virtues have been sung. . . .

Courage, it would seem, is nothing less than the power to overcome danger, misfortune, fear, injustice, while continuing to affirm inwardly that life with all its sorrows is good; that everything is meaningful even if in a sense beyond our understanding; and there is always a tomorrow. . . .

Joubert called the courage to be happy the most *beautiful* form of this supreme virtue. Certainly it beautifies its possessor, but it is also of all forms the most inspiriting to others. It does not ask for pity or even sympathy, but cheers. . . .

Charles Hamilton Aïdé, a late nineteenth-century writer, prayed "For calmness to remember, for courage to forget"—which comes close to the "courage to be happy." For obviously one cannot be happy while cherishing a grudge or nurturing a wrong. The "most beautiful form of courage" demands forgiveness—the "courage to forget. . . ."

But what—one thinks on—is happiness? Certainly it is not pleasure, though some people seem to think it is. I cannot help but think it is an inextinguishable sense of gratitude for and to life under even the most depressing circumstances. For there are no circumstances that can—or should—utterly blot out the recognition of goodness, the observation of beauty, and the memory of wonderful experiences. Happiness is a sort of continual act of faith, imposing a spontaneously accepted duty to be cheerful.

What We Make It

'TOWARD THE LIGHT'

For those who seek it, happiness abounds. In this selection from her book, Another Path, *author Gladys Taber tells how she finds happiness every day:*

My dear friend Faith has had in her life many sorrows and has achieved a tranquillity which might seem incredible. She also, being a very sensitive and caring person, has suffered with and for many others. We were talking one night about our lives and how to achieve the acceptance that leads to tranquillity. Faith told me, as we sipped our tea, that I tended to be impatient. Growth, she had found, is a slow thing and it is necessary to be patient with oneself.

I was reminded of another friend who wrote that even a year after the death of her loved one she still felt only bitterness. Nothing was any good, nothing mattered. Perhaps, I thought, her own sense that bitterness is not a good way of life is a first step toward trying to replace it. A small step, but a step nevertheless.

It seemed to me that Plato put it correctly when he

said, "Our eyes can be turned toward the light as well as toward the dark. If our whole soul is turned away from this visible world toward the bright regions, then our eyes can become able to understand the Good." He says further, "Do you not believe that it is a turning round of the soul into the right direction so that the eyes may see? For we all have eyes, though we do not know where to look."

I found these words lightened my hopeless hours. If I turned my soul in the right direction, my eyes could see. I saw a world in which I had some infinitesimal part, and to which I had an obligation. I saw the wide gaze of children, the tender look of lovers, the warm smiles of friends. I saw a newly opened rose. I saw the effortless flying movement of the Irish on a dewy lawn and the flat-out ears of the cockers following after. I saw so many wonders it would take a lifetime to list them.

By observing, my eyes saw the mysterious light of dawn and the still blaze of noon. I looked at the world—and I forgot myself. And I began to find some good in every day. I didn't try to work at being happy, I worked at finding that good in every day and experiencing it fully. And, at night, I thanked God in my prayers for whatever the good had been. It might be any one of a number of things: An unexpected telephone call from a friend. A letter of warm appreciation for something I had written. A neigh-

bor dropping in with a bouquet of pansies in mid-winter (from her small greenhouse). The sudden working out of a difficult problem in my current book. The overnight blossoming of the lilies of the valley. A special picnic with dear friends who only come on weekends. The voice of my granddaughter trying to get her tongue around words. "Tzeez," she says triumphantly, meaning "cheese."

There was, I found, something in every day if I kept my eyes turned toward the light!

CHARM

In her book That Certain Something, *actress Arlene Francis defines charm in terms of compassion and forgiveness:*

There is and must be a spiritual element in charm. It motivates the desire for understanding and the recognition that all of us are on this planet together, and not by our own request. I feel, too, that you can't detach charm from compassion. Compassion for the unhappy, the weak, and the underprivileged. And then there's one more step that might require a trained mountain goat and crampons to take: the capacity to forgive those who have harmed you and those whom you love.

CONFIDENCE

Confidence . . . thrives only on honesty, on honor, on the sacredness of obligations, on faithful protection and on unselfish performance. Without them it cannot live.

FRANKLIN DELANO ROOSEVELT

'THE GOOD LIFE'

According to poet Phyllis McGinley in her book, The Good Life on Earth, *happiness depends on expectations. Here she describes her formula for happiness:*

An unillusioned acquaintance of mine once said the good life was what other people seemed to live. I used to think in youth that it consisted of a constant explosion of joys, a succession of ecstasies, prizes, and great rewards. Now I realize all life is made up merely of days. And a good day is the most I dare define. Let it contain no unkindnesses, only a few homespun pleasures, and so far as a housewife like me is concerned, the soul can clap its hands and sing.

A good day is waking after eight solid hours of sleep to find the sun shining through windows that have lately been washed and curtains freshly laundered; and to know on the instant of rising exactly what to get from the market for dinner.

It is keeping an appointment with the dentist to learn, at the end of the ordeal, that one's gums are solid as cement and there isn't a cavity in sight.

It is picking up the mail at the back door to discover that instead of bills and throwaways addressed to Occupant, the postman has delivered a letter from a friend.

Perhaps the more ambitious of my sisters would name none of these mercies enough to make a day worthwhile; but they satisfy me. And there is a host of other daily good fortunes which can lift the spirit.

The papers may be full of wars and rumors of wars and disasters on land and sea. But they depress me only momentarily if household news is cheerful. I can go whistling down the stairs because of a compliment from my husband or a reaffirmation that my daughters are happy in their jobs and marriages. I can live brightly for a week on recollections of the Saturday party we attended where everyone was not only a friend but agreed with me about politics, books, morality, and the necessity of applying superphosphate to the soil around rose beds. The good life consists of such rejoicings.

For instance, this morning my day is already made by hearing from my younger daughter that Peter the Great, the smallest grandchild, is now taking a step or two even if totteringly; and that his older brother, Charlie, has been accepted by the nursery school of his mother's choice.

I am also elated by learning from the local library that the new mystery story so praised by critics is ready and waiting for me to take out. And pleasure has been further enhanced by my stepping on the scales to discover two pounds have delightfully drifted away.

What despairers forget is that our century is, in truth, not much more troubled than many another. In all ages the high-hearted have had to avoid as a constant preoccupation the wrongs and terrors of their epoch. I think now of Jane Austen, who, while England prepared to repel an invasion by Napoleon, wrote her witty and perfect novels, in which the severest crises were marriages, broken engagements, or an oversupply of houseguests. Which reminds me that Jane Austen is a serendipity all by herself. If a day has been unsatisfactory for me, it can be restored to pleasure by taking her down from a convenient shelf. Provided one does not ask for too much, the good life is frequently attainable.

'A GOOD DAY'S WORK'

Anna Mary Moses, in her book Grandma Moses, My Life's Story, *indicates life is what we make it:*

I have written my life in small sketches, a little today, a little yesterday, as I thought of it, as I remembered all the things from childhood on through the years, good ones, and unpleasant ones, that is how they come, and that is how we have to take them. I look back on my life like a good day's work, it was done and I feel satisfied with it. I was happy and contented, I knew nothing better and made the best out of what life offered. And life is what we make it, always has been, always will be.

HELPING OTHERS FORGET

A maid's simple observation gave Pavlova a personal goal in life. Here the famous ballerina relates the incident:

There are people who refuse to believe that a dancer's life can be otherwise than frivolous. But, in fact, the dancer's profession is altogether incompatible with a frivolous mode of living. If a dancer, yielding to temptation, ceases to exercise over herself the strictest control, she will find it impossible to continue dancing. She must sacrifice herself to her art. Her reward will be the power to help those who come to see her to forget awhile the sadnesses and monotony of life.

That much I realized, for the first time, at Stockholm.

34

In the crowd which escorted me when I left the theater, there were people of all stations: men and women belonging to the middle-class bourgeoisie, clerks and workmen, dressmakers' hands, shop assistants. They were all following my car, silently, and then remained standing in front of my hotel until I was told that they wished me to show myself on the balcony. As soon as they saw me, they greeted me with a stormy outburst of cheers which, coming after the deep protracted silence, sounded almost alarming. I bowed my head to them from time to time; and all of a sudden they started singing national tunes in my honor. I stood vainly seeking for a way of expressing my gratefulness to them. Then an idea struck me. I turned into my room, and came back with the wreaths and baskets of flowers which had been handed to me on stage. But even after I had thrown roses and lilies and violets and lilacs to the crowd, they seemed loath to retire. I was deeply moved and quite embarrassed. I could not help asking my maid, "But what have I done to move them to so great an enthusiasm?"

"Madam," she replied, "you have made them happy by enabling them to forget for an hour the sadnesses of life."

I never forgot those words. By speaking thus, my maid, a simple Russian peasant girl, gave me a new goal for my art.

'A LITTLE SOMETHING EXTRA'

Entertainer Eddie Cantor reveals his view of life in his book, The Way I See It. *Here he tells how he discovered the value of "a little something extra":*

As a kid on the lower East Side of New York, I used to run errands for all the women in our tenement. I could always count on a piece of home-made cake—a hunk of salami (salami was almost legal tender where we lived)—or even a few cents. It was a good deal, except that all of them insisted on sending me to the same grocery store—one that was ten blocks away.

There were five or six in the neighborhood which carried exactly the same stuff—so one day I switched. But only one day. They caught on—I couldn't figure out how—and when I got back, all I got was abuse.

Next time I went the ten blocks. And I would have gone *without* the threats. I was curious. What was so special about this guy? I'd seen him a hundred times and he looked like any other grocer.

Instead of wandering around the store, I watched him fill my order. He poured a quart of milk into the jug I'd lugged along—and then added a little more. My list read, "One dozen rolls." He counted out twelve—and threw in one more "for good measure." Instead of six bananas, he gave me seven. This character needed glasses! Feeling big-hearted, I pointed out his errors. But it seems they weren't mistakes at all. "It doesn't hurt to give a little something extra," he explained.

So that was his secret. "Give a little something extra." If it worked for him, why not for me?

In show business, those five words carried me from a Coney Island beer hall to starring roles on Broadway. And on Broadway, they really proved their worth. I was doing *Whoopee* when the market crashed. At the end of the strenuous first act, I really needed rest—but the audience was restless. Like every group in town, this one was full of "losers." I thought I might lighten some spirits—including my own—if I clowned around a little.

Everyone knew I'd taken a licking too, so I could crack wise without getting killed. I'd stand on stage and say things like, "That's not a white flag flying over Wall Street—that's Cantor's shirt." I told stories like the one about the guy who entered a large hotel and asked for a room on the nineteenth floor. The clerk inquired, "For sleeping, or for jumping?"

And people laughed. They may have had tears in their eyes, but at least I made them laugh for a little while. Night after night, I came out and kidded the crash. What else could you do except cut your throat?

Three weeks later, those off-the-cuff comments became the nucleus of my book, *Caught Short*. The first day out, it sold thousands of copies. Eventually, it went to 400,000. I recouped some of my losses, and made a lot of friends—all from "a little something extra."

I could go on and on with experiences of my own. I can't count the times that my crumbs cast upon the waters came back cake. However, the words inscribed on the Congressional Medal of Honor should be more conclusive than any of mine. This—our highest award—is only bestowed on one who distinguishes himself "above and beyond the call of duty." To the man who has given "a little something extra."

SOLITUDE

Author Anne Morrow Lindbergh emphasizes the value of being alone in this selection from her book, Gift From the Sea:

Solitude, says the moon shell. Every person, especially every woman, should be alone sometime during the year, some part of each week, and each day. How revolutionary that sounds and how impossible of attainment. To many women such a program seems quite out of reach. They have no extra income to spend on a vacation for themselves; no time left over from the weekly drudgery of housework for a day off; no energy after the daily cooking, cleaning and washing for even an hour of creative solitude.

Is this then only an economic problem? I do not think so. Every paid worker, no matter where in the economic scale, expects a day off a week and a vacation a year. By and large, mothers and housewives are the only workers who do not have regular time off. They are the great vacationless class. They rarely even complain of their lack, apparently not considering occasional time to themselves as a justifiable need.

Herein lies one key to the problem. If women were convinced that a day off or an hour of solitude was a reasonable ambition, they would find a way of attaining it. As it is, they feel so unjustified in their demand that they rarely make the attempt. One has only to look at those women who actually have the economic means or the time and energy for solitude yet do not use it, to realize that the problem is not solely economic. It is more a question of inner convictions than of outer pressures, though, of course, the outer pressures are there and make it more difficult. As far as the search for solitude is concerned, we live in a negative atmosphere as invisible, as all-pervasive, and as enervating as high humidity on an August afternoon. The world today does not un-

derstand, in either man or woman, the need to be alone.

How inexplicable it seems. Anything else will be accepted as a better excuse. If one sets aside time for a business appointment, a trip to the hairdresser, a social engagement, or a shopping expedition, that time is accepted as inviolable. But if one says: I cannot come because that is my hour to be alone, one is considered rude, egotistical or strange. What a commentary on our civilization, when being alone is considered suspect; when one has to apologize for it, make excuses, hide the fact that one practices it —like a secret vice!

Actually these are among the most important times in one's life—when one is alone. Certain springs are tapped only when we are alone. The artist knows he must be alone to create; the writer, to work out his thoughts; the musician, to compose; the saint, to pray. But women need solitude in order to find again the true essence of themselves: that firm strand which will be the indispensable center of a whole web of human relationships. She must find that inner stillness which Charles Morgan describes as "the stilling of the soul within the activities of the mind and body so that it might be still as the axis of a revolving wheel is still."

No Man Is An Island

THE POWER OF APPRECIATION

Author and counselor Dr. David Goodman is most widely known as a columnist, appearing in newspapers from coast to coast. Here he describes the power of appreciation—testimony to the truth that "no man is an island":

The self-centered . . . are always in a stew and a fret of personal hurt. So many things bother them. Every change of weather calls for a complaining comment, the government is corrupt, every businessman a crook, their friends false, their spouse unloving. They can't be talked to for fear of offending them. Everything pains them because they are set to feel everything in a personal way.

Those who keep free of self-centeredness by always seeing the good in people and things, escape the complainer's mess of misery and live full and satisfying lives. Thus the law of appreciation lifts us to a height of consciousness above the petty issues of the day and enables us to enjoy the good and avoid contact with the evil of life.

And unless we learn to apply this law, we are doomed to an existence of mediocrity, frustration, and defeat. For most of us, life is inherently limited. We have moderate means, we are bound to an ordinary job, we have little opportunity for travel or adventure, our folks are "just folks," and the one we marry is a merely mortal man or woman.

From this world of the commonplace, the law of appreciation rescues us. We enjoy our work, enjoy our friends, enjoy our families—in short, enjoy life. And we do it all ourselves by our power of appreciation.

What we appreciate is ours; what we belittle is lost, for we have, in effect, thrown it away. Appreciate more than you belittle, and you will live the abundant life; belittle more than you appreciate, and you will live a limited life. Such is life's spiritual mathematics, and any spiritual second-grader can figure out the good and bad results for himself.

Alas, that so many of us never got promoted out of life's spiritual first grade! For as appreciation is the beginning of spiritual life, so discontent is the beginning of death. Without appreciation, we are dull, brutish creatures. With it, we become as gods, literally creating a new world for ourselves, a world "a little nearer to the heart's desire."

Here the day is aglow with joy and beauty if we have the minds to see it. Don't let it sink into the night of apathy and gloom. Life calls on us to live this day and live it more abundantly. The sure means to this abundance is appreciation.

Remember always: *We draw unto ourselves the good of whatever we appreciate.* With this law alone, we can make our lives happy. With this law alone, we can make every day "the best day of the year."

DEMAND NOT

In her book You Learn By Living, *Eleanor Roosevelt warns that we must be able to accept the limitations of others:*

Just as we must learn to accept the limitations of others, so we must learn never to demand of someone else what is not freely offered us. This can apply to one's husband or wife, to one's children, particularly after they have left home, to one's friends. What is freely given in love or affection or companionship one should rightly rejoice in. But what is withheld one must not demand.

There are, of course, many ways of making such a demand, and the worst ways are not necessarily the overt ones, the open complaints, the querulous insistence. One can demand by implied appeals to sympathy and to duty, by pathos and helplessness and, in extreme cases, by illness.

This kind of demand is a form of spiritual blackmail and it sometimes develops into a ruthlessness, an emotional pressure which is essentially dishonest. It is not, unhappily, uncommon. People often refuse to recognize it in themselves. They regard themselves as abused, ill treated, neglected, everything, in fact, but what they are—attempting to get by force something that people are unwilling to give them. If they refuse to correct this tendency, then at least their victims must learn to resist steadily and firmly the assaults of this spiritual blackmailer.

'THE OPEN MIND'

Physicist J. Robert Oppenheimer was one of the most prominent developers of the atomic bomb. In a speech before a joint session of the Rochester Association for the United Nations and the Rochester Foreign Policy Association, he emphasized that all men must work together for "the hope of the future":

We need to remember that when the future that we can now foresee deviates so markedly from all that we hope and all that we value, we can, by our example, and by the mode and the style with which we conduct our affairs, let it be apparent that we have not abandoned those hopes nor forsaken those values; we need to do this even while concrete steps, to which we resort to avert more immediate disaster, seem to negate them. . . .

Each of us, recalling our actions in these last critical years, will be able to find more than one instance where, in the formulation or implementation of policy, we have been worthy of this past. Each of us will mourn the opportunities that may seem to him lost, the doors once open and now closed. Not even in critical times can the sense of style, the open mind, be fostered by issuing directives; nor can they rest wholly on soliciting great actions not yet taken, great words not yet spoken. If they were wholly a matter for one man, all could well rest on his wisdom and his sensitiveness—they neither are, nor can, nor should be. The spirit in which our foreign affairs are conducted will in the large reflect the understanding and the desires of our people; and their concrete, detailed administration will necessarily rest in the hands of countless men and women, officials of the government, who constitute the branches of our foreign service, of our State Department, and of the many agencies which now supplement the State Department, at home and abroad.

The style, the perceptiveness, the imagination and the open-mindedness with which we need to conduct our affairs can only pervade such a complex of organizations, consisting inevitably of men of varied talent, taste and character, if it is a reflection of a deep and widespread public understanding. That is why, despite their sketchiness, it has seemed appropriate to present these views to a group of interested and devoted citizens. It is in our hands to see that the hope of the future is not lost, because we were too sure that we knew the answers, too sure that there was no hope.

"The bamboo for prosperity," a Japanese friend explained to me, "the pine for long life, the plum for courage—"

"Why the plum for courage?" I asked, picturing courage as a great oak.

"Yes, yes," answered my Japanese friend. "The plum for courage, because the plum puts forth blossoms while the snow is still on the ground."

ANNE MORROW LINDBERGH

"Life begins tomorrow," says the Italian proverb. The secret is always to put much ahead of you; then you need not covet what you have left behind.

ARDIS WHITMAN

In the midst of winter, I finally learned that there was in me an invincible summer.

ALBERT CAMUS

IN DEFEAT

Actress Sarah Churchill, daughter of the late British statesman Winston Churchill, wrote this letter to her father following his party's defeat in 1945. She mentions the human qualities that made him the respected leader he was:

Darling, darling Papa,

You won't forget what you said last night about the Chartwell Colony, will you? No lovelier plot of land exists and there will be plenty of space and we could till the land and milk the cows and feed the chickens and you could have an enormous bell that you clanged when you wanted to see us, and when you did we would emerge from our little cottages and make our way down the valley. Some of us would cross the lake and we could all have an evening together and when do we really have better ones?

You were never more wonderful than last night. I am not half as good as you and Mama are about it. I am glad I went with you on one day of your great tour, I needed it for myself because I've been so hurt for you, so angry and bewildered at the violence and bitterness of the opening personal attacks on you by former colleagues, and the drive with you helps me now. Because after that day whatever convulsion has taken place I know that you are as high in their hearts as you ever were.

You know it is ironically funny, you know you were saying 'In war resolution, in peace goodwill, in victory magnanimity, in defeat defiance' well you taught me a great thing last night, in defeat humour. The other thing that has been running through my head is a bit out of my favourite prayer: 'To give and not to count the cost, to fight and not to heed the wounds, to toil and not to seek for rest, to labour and not to ask for any reward.' Well that certainly is your war record.

God bless you darling,

All my love to you and Mama.

'NOTHING TO FORGIVE'

April O. Armstrong writes about understanding and forgiveness in her book House With a Hundred Gates. *Here she describes her father, the late author Fulton Oursler, who exemplified these qualities:*

He made a creative art out of forgiveness and lack of resentment. Only once before his death did I ever see him unable to rally himself to ignore a hurt, and that time it was I who hurt him. I had assured him I would do something, and found I couldn't do it without hurting someone else whom I loved, and so I simply didn't do it. I didn't know what to say to him about it, so I didn't mention it, hoping he would understand, and, in the confused way of young people, hoping desperately that perhaps the whole thing hadn't been so important to him at all. It had been important. He didn't bring it up to me, but a deep slow sadness was spreading through his days, and in my heart I knew why.

I brought it up to him sidewise. He pretended not to notice. Then I asked him point blank if he was angry because of what I had not done. He denied it, not pettishly but truthfully: he wasn't *angry*. I told him then, simply, how I'd been caught in a dilemma choosing which person to disappoint, and that I felt badly about it.

As in a puff of smoke the sadness and bad feeling vanished. A dilemma he could understand. It was my silence that had puzzled him. No more need be said.

"Then you forgive me?" I asked.

"No." He smiled. "There's nothing to forgive. There almost never is, you know. I find it increasingly hard to forgive people because I find it increasingly hard to believe they've done me real harm, or done worse than I."

Forgiveness was for him . . . usually replaced by an unspectacular searching for his own faults. One person who constantly broke his heart by his apparent refusal to award him courtesy, let alone affection, I shall call Dudley. Dudley and my father had not gotten on for years. As long as I can remember, Dudley had taken all my father would give him, and asked for more. As long as I can remember, Dudley had quarreled and bickered, accusing my father of standing in his way, of looking down on him. Dudley particularly resented my father's conversion, and was making it his business to tell everyone that it had been simply another clever trick to advance a career, and a concession to my mother. All ventures of friendship on my father's part were rebuffed.

Dudley made me furious. Dudley made my father puzzled.

"I've failed him in some way," he said. "Not in the ways he accuses me of, but in something about me. He hates my guts. Hatred is an illness, and when people are ill they do and say things they don't mean. He means to hurt me, all right. But if he didn't hate me, he wouldn't mean to hurt me. The things he says I did to him didn't happen as he says. But there is a wound there."

That reasoning seemed specious to me, but it led my father to search his conscience and look at himself with Dudley's eyes. He selected from within himself the qualities which most offended this enemy. Then he wrote an article, disguising the facts of the case so no one could easily identify either Dudley or himself. In the article the narrator presents the circumstances of Dudley's meanness so that any reader is quickly led to despise Dudley. Then, as the article continues, narrator and reader both become aware of the personal flaws in the narrator which had alienated Dudley in the first place: a love of the limelight, a sense of self-importance, a need to excel and flaunt, the desire to offer advice and criticism, an unconscious inability to build up Dudley's ego for fear of jeopardizing his own. The narrator accuses himself of these flaws, and works fumblingly but diligently to overcome them. And in the article Dudley forgives him, and is no longer his enemy.

He entitled the article "The Hardest Lesson." It ran originally in a Hearst magazine and was reprinted later in an anthology of my father's work called *Lights Along the Shore*. He never told anyone what lay behind that article. I read it for the first time with tears in my eyes, recognizing its origin.

"Maybe the one you call Dudley will read it and recognize himself! He'll see how he underestimated you. Serve him right!"

Ruefully he shook his head at my excitement. "If he reads it he won't recognize himself or me. I didn't write it for him. I wrote it for me, and people like me. And you still don't understand, Dear. I don't want to serve him right. I'm serving someone else."

HAPPINESS

French author André Maurois discusses personal happiness in his book, The Art of Living. *The following selections offer insight into attaining a bright outlook on life:*

It is not events and the things one sees and enjoys that produce happiness, but a state of mind which can endow events with its own quality, and we must hope for the duration of this state rather than the recurrence of pleasurable events. Is this state actually an interior one, and can we recognize it otherwise than by the changes it produces in all exterior things? If we exclude sensation and memory from our thoughts, there is nothing left but a wordless emptiness. Where can pure ecstasy and pure happiness be found? As certain phosphorescent fish see the deep water, the seaweed, and the other creatures of the sea light up at their approach but never perceive the movable source of this illumination because it is in themselves, so the happy man, though he is aware of his effect upon others, has difficulty in perceiving his happiness and even greater difficulty in predicting it. . . .

"Do you wish to know the secret of happiness?" Several years ago in the agony column of *The Times* this question was asked, and all those who replied received an envelope containing two verses from

Saint Matthew: "Ask, and it shall be given you; seek, and ye shall find; knock, and it shall be opened unto you: For every one that asketh receiveth; and he that seeketh findeth; and to him that knocketh it shall be opened." Such, actually, is the secret of happiness, and the ancients had the same idea in another form when they declared that Hope was left at the bottom of Pandora's box when all the evils had taken flight. He who seeks love shall find it; he who devotes himself unreservedly to friendship shall have friends; only the man who desires happiness with his whole heart shall find it.

Early in life we put questions in an unanswerable form: "How am I to find the perfect man who deserves my love, or the unfailing friend who deserves my confidence? Where can laws be found which will assure the peace and happiness of my country? Where and in what occupation am I to achieve happiness myself?" No one can reply to those who state their problems in this way.

What are the questions that should be asked? "Where am I to find a person with weaknesses like my own, but with whom, thanks to our good intentions, a shelter from the world and its changes may be erected? What are the hard-won virtues necessary to a nation's existence? To what work can I devote my time and strength, thus forgetting my fears and regrets with the help of discipline? Finally, what sort of happiness shall I be able to achieve, and by whose love?"

There is no permanent equilibrium in human affairs. Faith, wisdom, and art allow one to attain it for a time; then outside influences and the soul's passions destroy it, and one must climb the rock again in the same manner. This vacillation round a fixed point is life, and the certainty that such a point exists is happiness. As the most ardent love, if one analyzes its separate moments, is made up of innumerable minute conflicts settled invariably by fidelity, so happiness, if one reduces it to its important elements, is made up of struggles and anguish, and always saved by hope.

LOVE

Famed psychoanalyst Erich Fromm describes love as an all-inclusive attitude. From his book The Art of Loving, *this selection differentiates love and "symbiotic attachment":*

Love is not primarily a relationship to a specific person; it is an *attitude*, an *orientation* of *character* which determines the relatedness of a person to the world as a whole, not toward one "object" of love. If a person loves only one other person and is indifferent to the rest of his fellow men, his love is not

love but a symbiotic attachment, or an enlarged ego-
tism. Yet, most people believe that love is consti-
tuted by the object, not by the faculty. In fact, they
even believe that it is a proof of the intensity of their
love when they do not love anybody except the
"loved" person. This is the same fallacy which we
have already mentioned above. Because one does not
see that love is an activity, a power of the soul, one
believes that all that is necessary to find is the right
object—and that everything goes by itself after-
ward. This attitude can be compared to that of a man
who wants to paint but who, instead of learning the
art, claims that he has just to wait for the right object, and that he will paint beautifully when he finds
it. If I truly love one person I love all persons, I love
the world, I love life. If I can say to somebody else,
"I love you," I must be able to say, "I love in you
everybody, I love through you the world, I love in
you also myself."

He who has not forgiven an enemy has not yet
tasted one of the most sublime enjoyments of life.

JOHANN K. LAVATER

Nature gives you the face you have at twenty; it is
up to you to merit the face you have at fifty.

COCO CHANEL

Worry a little bit every day and in a lifetime you will lose a couple of years. If something is wrong, fix it if you can. But train yourself not to worry. Worry never fixes anything.

MRS. ERNEST HEMINGWAY

I am an optimist. It does not seem too much use being anything else.

WINSTON CHURCHILL

Whatever I am is elemental and the beginnings of it all have their roots in Sawdust Road. I might have been born in a hovel, but I determined to travel with the wind and stars.

JACQUELINE COCHRAN

To be nobody-but-myself—in a world which is doing its best, night and day, to make you everybody else—means to fight the hardest battle which any human being can fight, and never stop fighting.

E. E. CUMMINGS

You gain strength, courage and confidence by every experience in which you really stop to look fear in the face. You are able to say to yourself, "I lived through this horror. I can take the next thing that comes along."

ELEANOR ROOSEVELT

I always wanted to be somebody. If I make it, it's half because I was game enough to take a lot of punishment along the way and half because there were a lot of people who cared enough to help me.

ALTHEA GIBSON

Self-respect cannot be hunted. It cannot be purchased. It is never for sale. . . . It comes to us when we are alone, in quiet moments, in quiet places, when we suddenly realize that, knowing the good, we have done it; knowing the beautiful, we have served it; knowing the truth, we have spoken it.

A. WHITNEY GRISWOLD

Happiness makes up in height for what it lacks in length.

ROBERT FROST

Humor is an affirmation of dignity, a declaration of man's superiority to all that befalls him.

ROMAIN GARY

Set in Linotype Aldus, a roman type with old-face character-
istics, designed by Hermann Zapf. Aldus was named for the
16th Century Venetian printer Aldus Manutius. Typography
by Grant Dahlstrom, set at The Castle Press.

Printed on Hallmark Eggshell Book paper.